the Colored page

Sundress Publications • Knoxville, TN

Editor: Sherrel McLafferty
Managing Editor: Tennison Black
Editorial Assistant: Kanika Lawton
Editorial Interns: Iqra Abid, Stephi Cham, Crysta Montiel, Neha Peri, and
Hailey Small

Colophon: This book is set in PT Serif

Cover Art: "the Colored page," by Jackie Liu

Cover Design: Kristen Ton

Book Design: Sherrel McLafferty

the Colored page

Matthew E. Henry
(MEH)

To the kids who made me capitalize "I" in my poems, and for Eche and Eric who demanded I make everyone call me "Dr. Henry."

"The instructor said,

> Go home and write
> a page tonight.
> And let that page come out of you —
> Then, it will be true.

I wonder if it's that simple?"
— Langston Hughes

Grateful acknowledgement is given to the following publications where these poems first appeared, sometimes with minor variations.

Baltimore Review: "mannish water"
Bending Genres: "when asked why they can't sing 'the N-word' in rap songs"
Biological Creatures: "an open letter for back to school night"
Brick [Rhetoric]: "my third grade teacher"
Bryant Literary Review: "an open letter to the white feminists holding a literary panel on Toni Morrison"
Gravitas: "an open letter to the school resource officer who almost shot me in my class"
Lucky Jefferson (Awake): "an open letter to the stupid [redacted] about to get [redacted] if they mention 'affirmative action' one more [redacted] time," and "revisionist history"
Massachusetts Review: "an open letter to the woman sharing her funny story in this writing workshop"
Mineral Lit: "when asked why Black people can't be racist"
Nightingale & Sparrow: "first grade mural"
Ninth Letter: "an open letter to my well-intentioned educators: past, present, and future"
Ploughshares: "twelve minutes a slave"
Poemeleon: "an open letter to the poetry editor of [name withheld on advice from counsel]"
Porcupine Literary: "an open letter to the secretary who asked how I haven't taken to drink or schedule 1 narcotics like so many of our colleagues," and "an open letter to the white girls caught chanting 'NIGGER' on Snapchat, again"
The Radical Teacher: "muscle memory," "the surprising thing," "when asked what I learned in elementary school being bussed from Mattapan to Wellesley," and "when asked why 'all lives' don't matter."
Rejection Letters: "an open letter to the public school employees worried that 'antiracist' is too controversial a term"
The Revolution Relaunch: "an open letter to the white teacher who threw a Black boy out of her class for wearing too much lotion," and "an open letter to those wondering why I've called this the most racist place I've ever worked"
Rigorous: "an open letter to an american institution," "an open letter to the young man on the subway platform, looking back, hurt and disgusted," "essay for history B," "etymology," "Little Africa," and "sailing Route 203"
Rise Up Review: "stop talking"
Shenandoah: "an open letter from the boy i was to the Man you have become"
Show Us Your Papers (Main Street Rag, 2020): "we all have to make sacrifices"
Solstice: "an open letter to my mixed little 'Sisters Who Kept Their Naturals'"
Syntax: "'only 300': a student's take on Harriet Tubman"
Tahoma Literary Review: "self-evident"

Contents

IV.

I.

"I am the only colored student in my class."
— Langston Hughes

when asked what I learned in elementary school being bussed from
Mattapan to Wellesley

what they think is appropriate: to treat Black hair
like a pregnant woman's belly, question if
larger nostrils enhance my breathing, probe my legs
for extra calf muscles under skin our teacher said
doesn't bruise because she can't see the blood-
screams beneath. I learned to tolerate

the frumpy lies of well-intentioned white women —
bosoms heaving, eyes liquid with Reaganomics,
Willie Horton and how they imagined my parents
as crack-whore mother and imprisoned father —
and their messianic attempts to save me
from my stable home. I learned to master

simon-says skills; to be a chameleon; to code-switch;
to bite my tongue instead of theirs; to make excuses
for them, yet allow awkwardness to pant circles around heads
asking what I prefer to be called *(Colored? Negro? African
American? Black?)* never landing on my name. I learned to execute

the affirmative action of elementary arithmetic —
$(\text{effort}^2 * \text{time})/x = \text{equity}$; that history is an art
painted in primary colors: white supremacy,
white privilege, white fragility; that darker shades are saved
for trees, rocks, dirt; that other tales struggle to sing
through the cacophony of the single story (slavery,
civil rights, poverty) muting a talented tenth;
that I should be grateful. I learned to accept

that "Cohen" and "Karelitz" were nigger-names before
my orange bus replaced their yellow stars; that kids
say the darndest things when grandparents remember
the Shoah, unlike others whose ancestors held whips
or felt pilgrim pride in the face of fallen feathers; I learned
to endure our words on their lips, when every bobby
and becky becomes *my brothah, my sistah*, teeth parted,
tongues already to the top of palates, waiting for the day
they can reclaim *my nigg...* I learned to drink

the cafeteria's chocolate milk, my back wall-braced;
to never trust sudden movements; to fight for every inch
of slide and swing, each papier-mâché turtle I "couldn't
have created on my own"; to recite *today's a good day
to die* — every day — down checkered halls to my seat
beside the office secretary, she who understood
the intersection of round pegs and square holes;
to enjoy solitary confinement recess; to admire the ants
who rebuild their lives after every collapsing storm
or malicious white sneaker. I learned

that they think I can't swim.

first grade mural

see the school swimming
along the blue felted wall.
a rainbow of identically
stenciled crepe paper.
a single eye. a crescent smile.

see the lone black fish
straddling the border
of the sea, shimmering
near the shore. a lone
Black fish, gasping for air.

Proverbs 22:6

how often did my Blackness
deny me what others my height
were afforded? the bent knees
lowering a furrowed brow
to my level. the gentle
white hand on my shoulder.
the lilting, *what's wrong, honey?*
the benefit of the doubt.

classical conditioning

we sit in our newly minted desks:
Melvin, Matthew, and Matt.
only three years from retirement,
she finds our names difficult
to distinguish. we bear no family
resemblance. two are Black.
one is white. when a question
is asked, and more than one
of our hands are raised,
we're never sure which she wants
unless she's smiling.

my third grade teacher

           explained skin,
the undercurrents
of blood, and how
my face lacked
the ability to bruise
or blush. I tried
to show her a patch
darker than the rest.
she nodded, explained
it was harder to see
on my skin.

a meditation on the ship *Desire*

we sat behind the driver smoking cigarettes,
the middle and high schoolers having already
staked their claim to the back of the bus. candy
clasped between thumb and two fingers, we mimed
uncles and street hustlers — snapping our wrists,
flicking invisible ash from cherry ends. blowing clouds
of powdered sugar, we mocked nancy reagan
and the nicest cop we'd ever meet in the suburbs
who told us to "just say no." something in her
joyless smile, something in the color palette
of his D.A.R.E. lessons, warned us
of the real war we were already fighting.

diaspora
for Dr. Q

she taught us more of Marcus
than Malcolm or Martin. to wish
upon *Black Stars*. to weep for a Zion
we never knew. to lift every voice and sing
words in a language she admits,
our ancestors never spoke.

("*Umoja* means 'Unity'!")

closeted away from our white peers,
we circle the table shrouded in kente colors —
the blues, golds, and greens, the maroons and yellows
she says clasp us to the breast of mother earth.
she asks if we can hear the choirs crying
from beneath the molasses sea, from beneath
the blood-soaked soil — songs in Hausa, Yoruba,
Ibo. many thousands gone. my attention

("*Kujichagulia* means 'Self-Determination'!")

ebbs, wanes. we're missing recess because
they said academic time can't be wasted. I understand
that I don't understand what she wants us to embrace.
don't fully see the connection between the cup, the candles,
the corn. I'm worried about what my parents will think:

("*Nia* means 'Purpose'!")

we're Christians. I doubt this would be approved
by *Focus on the Family* or *The 700 Club*. maybe
when I'm older...

("*Imani* means 'Faith'!")

we're missing recess.

mistaken identity

two decades later, when NPR mentioned
"the stewart heist," I saw how my father —
after bailing brothers out of Charles Street,
seeing nephews shackled in paddy wagons
outside Chez Vous — was found equally Black
enough to be stop and frisked, as BPD lynch-mobbed
through Mission Hill and Mattapan, Roxbury
and Dorchester. they meant the landscapes
and portraits. the *Artistic Soirée, The Concert,*
The Storm on the Sea of Galilee I underappreciated
on a fieldtrip the summer before fourth grade. not
"stuart" — the white-on-white crime, blamed on
the nearest Black faces. I remembered how
it would take three months for them to admit
what the lead detectives always knew:
it was an inside job.

early intervention

on September 21, 1990, *Boston Celtics* star rookie
Dee Brown exited a post office in Wellesley, MA,
where he was carjacked and brutally assaulted
by five police officers. making love to the pavement —
Glock 19s pointed at the back of his head —
they welcomed him to his new home:

an economic sundown community, a haven of white-
flight wealth, in which he should have known better.
his almost-wife — through hands as pale as theirs —
begged, until they recognized his name, that the amount
he allegedly stole was thousands less than what he made
the hour their jackboots remained pressed into his neck.

a year after the stuart hoax ended in the Harbor,
the dispatcher was told a Black man was standing
across the street from the bank robbed days before.
they weren't positive, but how many could there be
here, today, holding the mail, sitting in his car? waiting
for the slide, I learned about all this at recess.

johnny's mom signed the communal letter apologizing
for the damage done to the town's reputation (the handful
of Black residents appeared before the selectmen's board,
asked when their letters would arrive). sarah's father
thought everyone was blowing things out of proportion —
better safe than sorry. besides, no one was hurt.

self-evident

as a kid from Boston, the Revolutionary War
was my favorite subject in fourth grade.
a Tea Party I could respect. class trips vainly
searching for musket balls in Lexington treetops.
reading of decapitation by cannonball on Breed's Hill.
even the sights in Southie — unsafe for me to visit —
were a source of tribal pride. like rooting for the Patriots.

we were told to don our colonial imagination caps
and tell our story of emancipation from the British.
where would we be? the Old South Meeting House?
the Old North Church? what would we see as we rose
to American greatness? our teacher should hear freedom
ringing in the streets through our words. I dropped my head
to begin — oversized pencil in hand — until I remembered.

seeing my inaction, she crouched and began to re-explain.
I patiently waited for her to finish, eyes on her lips,
then asked if she wanted me to pretend to be white,
or to picture myself for sale on the steps of Faneuil Hall,
or stacked in one-half of the Harbor ships heading to
and from the West Indies, explaining my parents' *patois*.

after the vocal static — the hems and haws of white noise—
she suggested Crispus Attucks: the hometown boy, the Black
hero of the Boston Massacre. my siblings had taught me
the "one-drop rule," and when to nod my head politely,
so I pretended he was not half Wampanoag, that Framingham
was not his master's home, and imagined myself
the first unarmed Black man shot on these urban streets.

mannish water

when one of our new white neighbors asked
what he was eating and my mother — smiling
in Black, Gold, and Green — replied *curried goat,*
I saw visions of petting zoos and satanism
stroke the side of his face, the hand which held
his fork, before he turned and discreetly reached
for a napkin, searched for what looked anonymously
safe on the table. *ackee* and *saltfish. stew peas.*
callaloo. breadfruit. I saw the banquet spread,
the love-offering my family raised to be welcomed
into a New England suburbia whose gardens
are for show — not salads or tea. I heard
their names with paler ears. *bully beef*
and cabbage. tripe. chicken-foot soup. oxtail.

an open letter from the boy i was to the Man you have become

i don't remember what we even said. something
about your lack of femininity. *tomboy* at best.
lesbian at worst for a sixth-grade lunchroom.
you weren't a threat to me. had never attacked
my cultural insecurities. the new kid with too much
and too little of everything. the one used to richer whites
and poorer Blacks. having Rosenfelds and Ramsundars
as allies or buffers. your silence never made me feel
less than because my clothes, my music, my slang,
weren't fly enough. you were sitting when i followed them
to slap the sandwich from your mouth. a dare. a bet.
you barely flinched. this was an average Tuesday:
chicken tenders, american chop suey, fruit cup and
chocolate milk with a side of abuse familiar to us both.
but i saw the flash of surprise seeing my face with theirs.
before you dropped eyes to plastic tray, did you see the shame
only one of us still carries?

trial and error

he said we'd all laugh about this
one day, and excused Maria back to class.
a hand on my shoulder, he bailiffed me
out of his office and up the green-grey halls.

her smugness wrinkled into her shrunken face
when he told her the apology she sought
would pass her pale, grim lips, not mine.
Maria testified that she could not identify
exhibit A. was confused why she was summoned
when my name was clearly masking-taped
across the beige underside of my turtle.

thirty years later I remember the dog-eared
National Geographic filled with rainforest reptiles,
and the large white book borrowed from the library —
each culled to painstakingly match the color palette
of my mid-snap, papier-mâché masterpiece. I remember
the hours spent molding life to scale, perfecting
hexagons above a partially retracted tail. and

I remember her conviction that her suspicions
were reasonable, and my disrespect for her
snatching hands, thuggish. how my expulsion
from her seventh grade art class was justified
by my raised voice and unlikely talent.

an open letter to my vice principal from in-school suspension

thank you for teaching me the uselessness
of uplift suasion. to be more Malcolm
than Martin. to always hit back (or
first) if equal consequences come
no matter how polite I am, how many
cheeks I turn. since school doesn't differentiate
between the whys of Black bodies locked
in this room, and your zero-tolerance
flushes us all through The Pipeline
just as fast, I need to get my shots in early.

II.

"It's not easy to know what is true for you or me…
But I guess I'm what / I feel and see and hear…"

— Langston Hughes

essay for history B

I'm not a duly elected representative of Niggerdom
who's authorized to speak for all my people everywhere.
but that's exactly how you see me, expecting house negro hands
to eagerly raise and answer your every classroomed question.
to play mammy and educate massa's children. to do your job
in the shortest month, or when topics turn to Atlantic currents,
brown sugar and people. Harriet and Sojourner. Booker T and W.E.B..
Malcolm and Martin. Biggie and Tupac. you see me when convenient.
when you want me to drink your 2% curriculum, say thank you, and smile
showing all my teeth. but when I won't consent to be your magic negro —
when I raise my hand to discuss the beast on my block, the knees
which find our backs for walking in your neighborhood, the pistols
pointed center mass because my father's taillight was out —
you silence me with threats of slipping grades, or calling officer whitman,
without seeing how this too sings of america. sometimes, it seems,
you do not want to be a part of me, or learn from me — younger
and Black and somewhat less free. you should know, the feeling is mutual.

context

because I made the mistake
of paying close attention
to our teacher's droning on

about Holden Caulfield's
existential plight
of common white privilege,

I was never sure of the story
you were telling — whether
you stage-whispered

> *lynch that fucking nigger,*
>   or
> *Lynch, that fucking wigga*

to the other slackers hanging
on your every word, before
she turned her back to the board,

and regained order.

we all have to make sacrifices

another black-clad, brown haired white boy has shot-up his school.
40 miles away, two counties over, but it's my name and picture
they've laminated, noosed about my neck. I waste an extra 20 minutes
every morning to prove I bear the name my mother gave me,
am not one of the other God-tanned she can't tell apart. chastised
for talking in line, for moving *too slow* by a matronly bouncer
at the worse club in town. *you need to have your ID ready.*
have you never been to an airport? probably not. her doubtful eyes
flicker between my face and the plastic facsimile in her hands —
changing the angle, catching the light fourteen times, once
for every bullet that disrupted class, was sent home in bone and blood.
asking, *why you people can't just keep your hair consistent*
with what's in the photo? it should be a law, before wondering
if my sigh is reasonable suspicion to search my book bag because
you never know. but every day I'm the one *holding everybody up,*
stopping them from getting an education. after a final squint,
my algebra teacher from last semester will shove back my lanyard,
shoo me along, and greet haleigh with a smile, comfortable knowing
she's doing her part to keep us all safe.

twelve minutes a slave

we held a slave auction in class today —
probably not a state-sanctioned component
of AP U.S. History. but Mr. S made a block
out of the front row desks, cordoned it off
with backward facing chairs. he shame-forced
Tony Miller above us, introduced him
as "item #5." he'd prepared a catalogue:
a one-sided sepia sheet with Tony's description
and a starting price. before the bidding,
Mr. S made Tony turn in perfect circles
"so we could all see what we were getting."
made him show his gums and teeth, roll up
his sleeves and flex, lift an Oxford Unabridged
over his head and strain for as long as he could.
we were encouraged to holler — not yell —
intrusive questions about Tony's pedigree
and prior owners. to discuss if he was better suited
for house or field. to speculate about breeding options.
after Tony climbed down — unable to meet our eyes
or the oppressive silence — I was almost ashamed
that a white teacher treating one of his own like this
made my Brown skin rattle with the joy of falling chains.

nah, I'm good

yes girl, it's me. 154 pounds of taut muscle
showing almost everything my momma gave me.
the Brown bomber who just beat your current classmate's
back into the second round wrestling mat. I see you
seeing me — eyes widening with recognition,
lip biting with desire for the one you now think
got away. but I never forgot third through fifth grade:
the notes checked "no." the obligatory Valentines
you always ran out of. the friend you sent
to ward off my crush.

yes girl, you're right to stall your approach —
to pocket the half-wave I never got when
it mattered — while I reconnect with others
who shared our swing-sets and glitter sticks,
until I moved away and beyond you. save
that sad, slight smile for someone who cares
about the letterman's jacket absent your shoulders,
or your flip-phone's silence this close to prom.

conversation with a white girl

so, you're Colored right?
this after asking me to
her prom. the year
'97. there are no words
to describe why: I said *yes.*

the decade we won't discuss

how your laughter first slapped my face — too Black
for your father, not Black enough for you.
breaking into my gym locker, leaving
flowers and a suicide note. faking
seizures at 3 am so I'd hold you
shaking in emergency rooms. the fist-
holes you placed in the wall. the smashed teapot.
swearing I'd move across the country and
marry a lesbian I'd never met.
the caffeine pills. the confessions. the shard
of glass still in my hand. the ring. that night
in the Burger King parking lot. the day
you threatened to kill yourself if I left.
the faked pregnancy. the morning after.

overexposure

see the hand raised to a thoughtful chin,
a pencil erasing whimsical mistakes.
head tilted away from the camera,
a filter highlights high-definition waves,
wool they could reach out and touch.

see how the half-smile stops
at his thick, siren lips — closed, but lying
as they always do in every photo
suggesting campus diversity.

Western Heritage

she asked, *what grade were you in
when you had your first Black teacher?*

suddenly I'm sprinting down sepia halls,
through pastel classroom doors, tracing
the corners of my mind, scanning from wall
to wall to see who stands in front of the black
then green then white board. across forty years,
five towns and disciplines, the reel spins — crayons
to pencils to pens to keyboard, from poetry
to prose and back — until I see him

teaching history my freshman year of college,
a decade before I stood in the same spot.

conversation with a white girl

historically, Blacks
had it better than women.
true as second-class
citizens. she forgets: once
I was legally livestock.

sailing Route 203

it was the casual racism of white women who trusted me —
how consistently they relayed their fathers' fears for their safety —
that piqued my interest, opened my eyes on this stretch of road
where Gallivan Boulevard turns to Morton Street. how black-
top turns treacherous, fills with basilisks and dragons pushing
toward the edge of their liquid world. how pale drivers never
lift eyes from taillights or stray beyond serrated lines.
how white knuckles kraken-clutch 10 and 2, lest souls be snatched
from seats by Scylla or Charybdis — Jamal or D'Vontaye —
at every flash of yellow on the horizon (and how they fear the red!).
how I can almost hear teeth grinding in jaws over the sound
of an already locked door desperately trying to re-engage again
and again and again, windows scraping upward like sea glass over
Leviathan's scales. how their backs straighten in safe waters,
rowing bold once they hit the Arborway feeling they've tamed
the narrow green serpent wanting to throw their weight off
her fearful back. how furtive glances become naked aggression
as property values rise and dark monsters submerge in the rearview.

an open letter to an american institution
after Kooser

when first I visited "Fort Robinson" —
where four stanzas croon casual slaughter,
average hands about most savage work —

I saw the *american dream* thrown face down
in the grass. a knee in its back. beaten
like nestling magpies. a clot of feathers. blood-

matted beneath rope-like limbs. from porches,
mothers keen for the breathless fallen. as some
flee before a most blue and red winter,

others turn their backs to capture selfies.
tell me Ted, does your boy — safe in your car
and color — cry when he sees the same today?

conversation with a white girl

I'm fine officer!
he left disappointed:
sorry, no rape rescue.
but she remained incensed at
this insight into real life.

an open letter to my marxist classmate in philosophy 102

no: I'm Black
first. because

your eyes work
in conjunction

with a Kantian analytic
already prescribing who,

what, I am when you see
me; all other sense data —

synthetic,
a posteriori —

require my participation
in your experience:

to which imperatives
I bend a knee; my thoughts

on what's beyond
the numinous veil;

which vocation staves
off existential angst;

with whom I may couple
sexually; the number

of spaces reserved
in my basement

beside the others
who asked the same.

an open letter to the boys who screamed "go back to Africa" at
Wheaton College (MA), Fall 2003

thank you.
        your drunkenness
dragged my ears captive
on the perfect night.
the knife forgotten in my car
made every branch and rock
a manslaughter
from which to later
wipe blood and prints.
and I was thankful
for the chance
to whip massa's sons.
to blow off steam
on slurring college boys
who fit the description.
thankful for the wish
fulfillment: a proverbial
motherfucker who would.
thankful for a night
to learn which white friends
would turn on a dime,
fall in line beside.
were willing to call home
for our bail money.

III.

"Well... / I like to work, read, learn, and understand life."
— Langston Hughes

an open letter to the secretary who asked how I haven't taken to
drink or schedule 1 narcotics like so many of our colleagues

my inward rolling eyes consider the twenty-six administrators in seven years,
including the principal who put a pregnant woman in a headlock, who said *i
gave the Hispanics a soccer ball, what more do they want?* another arrested for
battering his wife. the week it took for IT to realize our new emails said *pubic
school.* the budget cuts and bomb threats. fire drills, tornado drills, chemical
spill drills. the porn accident in physics class. the students discussing which
of us would take a bullet with their names on it, later seen in handcuffs,
cages, caskets. the cancers and car crashes. the substitute who dropped her
panties and shat on the wheelchair ramp inside the library. the teacher caught
shirtless with a 14 year-old in her car. the sleepless nights holding secrets like
hands after abortions, miscarriages, and becoming a godfather. I don't know
how to answer, save showing you a blank page and a pen filled with blood.

an open letter for back to school night

your child was sexually assaulted at a party
almost — a friend intervened as sober hands
fumbled against an impaired zipper. your child is in love

with sharp edges — clothespins, safety razors, and
exacto-knives wait red-spotted under the bed, but
your maid has yet to notice. your child hasn't eaten

solid foods in three weeks, has slit both wrists
in frenetic dreams, takes whatever colored pills
are closest to hand, drinks until feelings can't be felt.

your child found your Tinder profile, your stash,
the photos, the manila envelope containing the truth.
your child overheard you that night, hears

what you really mean, even though you're too afraid
to admit it. your child has told me these things because
you're too busy posting shit about other parents on Facebook

and they don't want to be a distraction.

an open letter to my classmate on a conversation we never had

you sat across from me on the Red Line. somewhere
between Park Street and MGH — as the morning crush
of suits and scrubs dispersed — I noticed our book
in your hands. the grey cover held together
by a rainbow of "used" stickers, the pages jaundiced
by highlights, the time-wrinkled spine all matched
the one in my bag. I smiled, but only to myself.
I knew we were on the same track, heading toward
our first day of ice breakers and imposter's syndrome.
how our cohort would spend semesters sharing study notes
and nightmares. discussing quantitative approaches
to statistics and religion. complaining about qualifying
papers while celebrating pregnancies. we would support
each other through dissertations and divorces, diplomas
and deaths. but I kept all of this to myself. I knew better.
just as I knew how long I should wait before exiting the train
at our stop and to use a different door. knew to eschew
getting my steps in to make you more comfortable, enduring
the glacial ascent of Porter's escalator. knew to ignore
how you clutched your purse and sped up when — entering
the same building — my presence behind you was unavoidable.
knew how to bite my tongue when, in class, you teared up
explaining the implicit bias and micro-aggressions discussed
in our grey book.

an open letter to the young man on the subway platform, looking
back, hurt and disgusted

carrying a book with its spine unbroken
is the new "whistling Vivaldi" —
a safer way to assuage
the angst of white women
who walk in a world
of Black men in public spaces.
more powerful than a smile
or an expensive suit.
it catches them off-guard.
reflexively unclutches
their purses. try it.
see how their eyes train
on your hands
to sate their curiosity —
to judge the tatterless cover —
before they track up
and refocus:
the apparition
on a Brown bough
transforms
into your face.

small world

the moment he went silent, I knew. but I'm an asshole
who can't help himself.
                your family lives in Wellesley?
it's not a question. we were having an almost pleasant
conversation about equity in curriculum development
and classroom management. almost.
                what elementary school did you attend?
though my graduate student, we're well within
the seven-year window of swing sets and soccer balls, number-sense
and long division. hate to see a grown man squirm but,
like I said: I'm an asshole. his parents spent the extra cash
and social capital on a private school education because
his future couldn't be risked under the "bad influence"
of "those Black kids from Boston."
                tonight, before mommy tucks you in,
                and daddy whispers how special you are, tell them
                how much they're now paying for the privilege.

submitted for your approval

I am uploading this article response two hours
after observing one of my student teachers,
and her overly maternal, handle like fragile-
fine-crystal care of a second grader in her class.
when asked, she relayed the story of how his mother
zombie-shuffled into the classroom during snack
strung-out on heroin. how she proceeded to swear
at the bookshelves and pet iguana, searched cubbies
for sellables, and then passed out on the friendship rug
in front of a gasping class and her mortified son—a child
she required, upon awakening, to brace her to the office
before the ambulance, the police, and his father could arrive.

social services were called. reports were filed. but
after two weeks, no home visits were scheduled because,
I quote, "the mother would not return their phone calls."
when she refused to get clean, his father kicked her out.
she responded to the injustice of natural consequences
by breaking in, stealing her son's Xbox, and selling it
for a flight of fentanyl. her current whereabouts are unknown
creating a problem because, being only the "baby daddy,"
his father is unable to sign school forms, like the IEP
replacing the one she destroyed in a lethargic fit of rage.
but for the first time in two years, this boy has attended
nine straight school days, and everyone is ecstatic.

with this in mind, I drove back to my office
and began our assigned reading. I know this
is not the response you were expecting but,
respectfully, I can't give one good God-damn
about action research into the effectiveness
of mindfulness practices on district-level administrators
in Villa Park, CA.
                    nor should I ever.

an open letter to the stupid [redacted] about to get [redacted] if
they mention "affirmative action" one more [redacted] time

sometimes I miss the daily reminders
that they hadn't hired "a colored person"
in 40 years. how that bedroom community
of Boston took pride in their pronounced
klan presence. the perks of working
in a building where the vice principal
refused to shake my hand.

sometimes I miss the diversity of rural life:
where the only "others" were also imported
to that summer destination in New Hampshire.
the balance of perpetual autumnal colors, and
students unafraid to openly call me "nigger."

sometimes I miss being the only Black professor
in a program where I was once the only Black face
on the website for over a decade, wondering if my legacy
will be passed to the lone Brother sitting in my old seat.

but now I work in a suburb which provided
a police escort — for winding miles in my rear-view —
to an interview where I was asked, repeatedly,
if I would remain longer than the other minorities
hired once upon a time.

"Little Africa"

        they called it. the heart
of darkness. the dark continent
in the middle of the cafeteria's sea,
where all the Black kids sit. just as
drs. livingston and Tatutm
would rightly presume.

when asked why I changed my seat at this faculty mixer

because you — a grown-ass,
forty-something, white woman
with an advanced degree, who daily
works with students of color — said
a senior in high school — 17,
white, male — had to explain to you
why blackface, yellowface, and
brownface are wrong — always,
including Halloween — last —
God-damn — week.

an open letter to the white teacher who threw a Black boy out of
her class for wearing too much lotion

his skin was ashy. perhaps that's a concept
you're unfamiliar with — like seasoned chicken,
leaving vegetables out of Jell-O molds, and
salads not solely composed of acai, goji berries,
and candied almonds. but we whose flesh knows
what it's like to hunger and thirst, will not be whitened
like a glass of whole milk.

you call his basic Black hygiene insubordination,
his social survival disrespect. because you have allergies
and say one whiff of him might make you sneeze?
given the lifetime of nose-holding he'll have to endure,
can't you do the same for 64 mins? and if your curriculum
is so unimportant sitting his moist elbows in the hallway
doesn't impact his grade, the next round of budget cuts
are yours to shoulder.

and while I have your attention: stop touching,
smelling, touching, back-hand complimenting,
touching Black girl hair — your brown-rooted blonde,
drowned-poodle locks are no reasons to assault
the magic of their coco-buttered curls.
and another thing...

an open letter to my mixed little "Sisters Who Kept Their Naturals"

my dears,
                    I love you because a hot comb
never dared to look you in the eye. because
your lives are always in autumn — a crisp,
stern season of self-awareness. because
you stroll through the background radiation
of racial anxiety without a hazmat suit. because
you have desired to be darker and lighter,
invisible, yet star-shine. because
you hold and withhold, extending yourself
with eyes older than a million years. because
you consult a social color-palette — carry skin-swatches
to know which suburban parties are safe. because
you two-step between both worlds
and always make it home. because
you stand erect beneath a gaze which finds you not exotic,
but spicy white or unseasoned black. because
you are more acceptable to fathers and mothers
who feel one side sanctifies the other, explains
something significant about their sons. because
you have not fully bought into their blonde lies,
and get heated when every marilyn and farrah,
chloe, kim, and becky worship your hair
on themselves. how they adore and imitate,
but never testify to its source, never ask to touch
the curls they claim. my dear little sisters, I celebrate
that your rough, darkish music is othered because
it is right and real and deserving the natural
respect of self and the sea.

an open letter to the white feminists holding a literary panel on
Toni Morrison

look to your left, your right — where
are her sisters? why are they missing?
while there's a shared violence only
your bodies can know, they were never
your breasts from which milk was stolen
or freely given to sons with their own
white teeth. your daughters will never
destroy dolls, scraping skin to find the beauty
beneath. will never see their fathers shot
off fences, or shucking with shirley temples
while they watch from behind grim windows.
you will never slit throats as a slave-act
of salvation, or place a God-tanned pap
between gums with uncertain futures. your backs
are forever clear of chokecherry trees. you —
whose faces adorn the cups, the magazines,
the movies — are married to the master
narratives she subverts. are intrusive
as rusty nails breaking an arch. move
her stilled lips without consulting her face,
her family. forget she still has a voice.

an open letter to the woman sharing her funny story in this
writing workshop

the pair of gold teeth you found as a child, hidden
at the bottom of your mother's jewelry box,
were not from your father's dental school failure,
artificials he filed from ferric molds. they were —
as you believed them, secreted in your hands —
strip-mined from someone's mouth. remember
the confusion over how to pronounce your last name.
the mystery of your people arriving in Saint Cloud
by way of Argentina. the paternal grandparents
who go unmentioned. the elderly man — a number
screaming from beneath his slipped sleeve — clutching
the sides of your head outside the grocery store.
how he stared at you with a horrible questioning,
seeing something familiar in your face.

an open letter to the poetry editor of [name withheld on advice
of counsel]

please don't revise my poem to make my Blackness
worthy of dating your daughter — inoffensive and less centered
in ways that make you clutch the pearls and purse
you thought it was eyeing. don't evict its diction —
tear down and rebuild — so you can sublet my stanzas
for artisanal mayonnaise. this isn't Brooklyn. though
you've worked with Rankine and Hayes, Clifton and Kaur,
Willis-Abdurraquib and Walker, your suggested title
almost made me wonder if you have hooded sheets.
yes, I meant *axed* and *aight*, just as much as I intended
antediluvian and *assiduous*. I'm sorry, but your cute anecdote
about Representative Lewis won't replace my allusion
to Huey P. Newton. and those final images are "stark"
and "disquieting" because I lived them. my immigrant mother
lived them. my student — a raisin floating in a bowl of milk —
lives them. every day. look, I know what my piece was wearing
when she left the house — she was appropriately dressed
for the occasion and did not need to slip into something
you would find more comfortable. but thanks for the feedback.

IV.

"I guess you learn from me..."
— Langston Hughes

when asked why I stress the "Dr." after swearing I wasn't about
that life
> *for Eche*

"you're one
of the only
       Black men

with those letters
behind your name
that They
      may ever see —
that We
      may ever see.

make sure
They put some
        Respect

on it."

revisionist history

"...You put a nigga in Star Wars. Maybe you need two, and then,
maybe then we'll believe you see Black people in the future..."
— "Black America Again," Common

Common's clever rhymes
bred online discussions about Hollywood
tokenism and progressive post-racialism
amongst the hip-hop intelligentsia.
              while some argued
the count across the entire franchise —
the number of named brothers, no sisters,
who wielded lightsabers and X-8 night snipers
on the screen — Blerd that I am, my first thought
was about the anachronism. that the whole
space opera took place — past tense —
"a long time ago, in a galaxy far, far away,"
calling into question the whole conceit.
              but then I considered
the curriculum we teach. the slim books
stacked like hulled bodies in the back
of my classroom — *Uncle Tom's Cabin,*
Huckleberry Finn, Things Fall Apart
A Raisin in the Sun, The Bluest Eye, Citizen.
I thought maybe They need to see Us —
We need to see Us — on different ships,
in different positions: captains and pilots
              instead of cargo.

"only 300?": a student's take on Harriet Tubman

he was incredulous in that pure white
bread, middle-class way I've learned
to make excuses for. in his estimation
she hadn't done enough. the math
was in his favor: she left many behind.
thousands gone.

in the back of the classroom I sit, quietly
observing his bottled tan and bleached dreads.
knowing how quickly his car stereo descends
in contrast to his driver's side window
when adjacent skin of a darker hue.

pine for poor Harriet: her handgun,
her pointless heroism, her foot ferry
failure, her star treks lost without
syndication on MTV or streaming
on Netflix. yes. "only 300." I hear you

my young, white brother. I hear you.
now shut the fuck up and sit down.

stop talking

sitting in a colleague's class, listening to
high school students compare a Christian baker
denying wedding cakes to same-sex couples,
to Black men asked to perform a song and dance
for the KKK. the hypothetical caused
some to glance at my skin, my silence. from behind me
one young man explained the klan didn't exist
anymore, hadn't killed anyone in decades
according to his impromptu estimation.

        this
after Mother Emmanuel, where nine closed eyes,
folded hands in prayer, and opened to Jesus.

        this
after tiki-torch Nazis crashed hateful white waves
of clubs and cars into peaceful bodies.

        this
as freedom flyers arrive in mailboxes, daily
making white pride promises of protection
and a good night's sleep despite the encroaching
darkness.

    it wasn't my class, but I slowly turned
to make the only appropriate contact I could —
Stop talking, a finger slicing across my throat,
miming the tracks of chains, knives, nooses.
he tried to make it better. began to explain...
No. Stop talking. he did.

       I should have said more.

"Middle Eastern countries can't sustain democracies"

the last thing I expected to hear from your D-
in social studies mind on a Monday morning.
but here we are, in the school library
listening to you opine on geopolitics.
please: tell us more about how everyone
is always shitting on Schrödinger's international
constable — the United States simultaneously
being and not being the world's police force.
about how those camel jockeys should be grateful
we haven't bombed their wasteland holy places into
parking lots. about how dictatorships
or terrorists are the only practical options
for backward savages stuck in the 1800s,
who wave nuclear weapons like a child with his
rusted scimitar demanding to be taken
seriously. I'd laugh at the irony
except your future as a titan of industry —
a political lion — has already been purchased
by your parents. so it was surprising when a Brown
friend — whose family hails from the lands you hate —
approached your table, and you fell silent.

re: your aryan princess in my class

dear Mr. and Mrs._____,
                              I am writing to inform you
about your failure. your daughter,
a 10th grader in my class, raised her hand
and asked — out loud — what "race" she is. undoubtedly
this comes as a great shock. I'm sorry to report
the white supremacy you have patiently sown,
watered and sunned, has fallen on fallow soil.
this may be related to her inferior inference skills
and utter lack of reading comprehension of social cues.
the first-cousin connection between you two
may also play a role. regardless of the cause,
I felt it was in her best interest to make you aware
that no matter how well stocked your bunker
with assault weapons, MREs, and Pabst Blue Ribbon,
she is uncertain of her side once the race war starts.
while the South may rise — your sheets duly bleached
and pressed for such an occasion—she's in danger
of being sought out as collateral damage
by your more stalwart disciples of david duke.
the Southern Cross beside your MAGA
bumper sticker will not be sign or sigil enough
to ward off their advances. I strongly suggest
you invest more energy in imparting your white ways.
time better spent than arriving at my office door
to complain about an anticipation guide about identity
in *The House on Mango Street.*

etymology

"white" is not an adequate ethnic label in America. but "Black" is. it often falls to me — their "Black teacher" — to explain. we were raised from ship hulls on hooks, pried loose from the rigid dead, spoons unstacked from the bent, the rusted. we were traded on commercial winds. copper and cloth. rum and molasses. tobacco and hemp. last names more honest, more telling, than Washington. Johnson. Henry. Freeman. Freedman. Brown. others have acknowledged pasts, are allowed a hyphenated heritage. can add "American" to the end of anything. Irish. Italian. German. Dutch. French. there is no need for "white" unless making a statement, a distinction. like separating laundry. or water fountains. but our Ur-nation is undiscovered. seven possible ports are not a country. so we are known by our hue (Colored, Negro, Black) or remain caught in the middle, the passage between whole continents (Africa, America).

when asked why Black people can't be racist

because words have meanings that don't change
based on how they turn your stomach. because,
despite the inequity of the fledgling guilt you feel,
our losses are never the same. because racism
is a rigged game of Monopoly where you're both
the race car and the top hat. and you begin
with your $1500 dividend doubled. and the banker
is your doting grandmother, who has already co-signed
all your deeds and developments, and set aside an extra
$400 for whenever you pass GO. and Reading Railroad
is pronounced however the fuck you want it to be
though it was built by other hands. and control
over the utilities was assured by your third trip
around the board. and every day is a tax holiday,
but only for you. and when you finally hand the dice
to the thimble, you fail to notice how every Chance
card contains a fine. how the Community Chest
is always closed. how I receive a citation for loitering
on Free Parking and 40 lashes just visiting jail.
how my rent triples regardless the number of homes
or hotels you may have. and when, through hard work,
scheming or an accidental blessing, I find myself
in possession of Park Place, the doorman still asks to see
my ID and calls the police (which you also own). so if
in frustration I deny you service at my singular hotel,
sully your white walls and stiff brim with mud, or
sweep the board with a righteous right hand, cursing
the whiteness of money bags, bubble-letters, and you,
it may not be comfortable, but it's not "racism."

connotation/denotation

when asked why they accepted
their physics teacher's assurances
that their elementary understandings,

their dictionary definitions of "gravity"
were so simplistic they skirted lies —
falling apples and attractive bodies — but

refused to acknowledge the same in this case,
despite scores of screaming sociologists,
his quiet honesty shifted the ground beneath us:

because being wrong about gravity
doesn't make me feel bad about myself.

when asked why "all lives" don't matter

                              ...after a deep breath,
I attempted to explain. my aunt had breast cancer.
despite a healthy dose of science and Scripture,
prayer and prescriptions, the shadows never dimmed.
we celebrated her life, mourned the hole her grave
dug in ours. we lauded her lovingkindness, questioned
the natural shocks flesh is heir to — why this disease
would claim a wife, a co-worker, a friend, an aunt.
at the repast heads turned to the future: saving
other sons and daughters, ourselves. a collection was taken
to fund breast cancer research. a medical scholarship
for oncology study discussed. a proposal for new
from the back of the church hall, a woman no one recognized
screamed, "what about ovarian cancer?! and prostate cancer?!
why aren't you all talking about those? all cancers matter!"

most of my students nodded into the ensuing silence. but some
blank stares and my job description doomed me
to be more didactic: to explain appropriate time, place, and manner,
intent versus impact, the guilt and shame required
to derail communal grief and hijack a narrative
to make oneself more comfortable.

I explained the human duty to choose:
enter the room willing to bear bodies on our shoulders,
or, arms empty, leave and silently stand outside.

I said, "replace 'cancer' with 'lives'" and waited.

an open letter to the school resource officer who almost shot me in
my class

was it the loud noises which drew your attention,
commotion you couldn't process fourteen months
from Afghanistan? a threat too quickly assessed
through the two by three window of my classroom door?
was it my Brown arms gesturing wildly, or my beard —
long and unkempt — which obscured thick lips
releasing a language you couldn't easily decipher
(aggarwayter. pillory. Defarge.)? was that what triggered
rules of engagement normally absent halls so affluent?
did I seem out of place? did you not notice my shirt and tie?
the matching slacks, socks, and shoes? could you not see
the books open beneath mostly white faces? the smiles
which faltered with your entrance? many missed
your sidearm's slide back to safety as you stumbled
to silence when asked if I could help you. the two
who share my skin saw everything. made eye contact.
held it for two solid seconds. the next day they took
to calling me "almost Tamir," while your near-miss
story was met with laughter in your squad room.

when asked how I ended up in the principal's office

after reading *The Dew Breaker*,
and to stay with Danticat,
we circled back and read
"Message for my Daughters."
I had to explain Amadou Diallo
and Abner Louima and Oscar Grant.
they (vaguely) remembered the name
Trayvon Martin (something about Skittles
and hoodies), as much as they understood
that on that day, on that playground,
Tamir Rice was exactly their age
for those twelve seconds.
Rekia Boyd and Sandra Bland
were blackholes to their minds,
as was Walter Scott. but they had no excuse
for Botham Jean and Atatiana Jefferson
and Ahmaud Arbery (and whoever else
will join the list before we finish this conversation...
Breonna Taylor...George Floyd...).
the usual suspects spoke up, too loudly
and for too long. I locked eyes with the devils
advocating an excuse for lynchings,
and pointed at their supposed Black friends.
pointed at myself. asked would I still be alive
if I just knew my place?

a confession from occupied territory

after the frantic emails — a cry for help in the middle of a night
one student feared another would not survive — I called the police,
resisting the screaming of my skin. after weighing the sharp,
bloody consequences of inaction, the cost of action crushed
my chest. I couldn't breathe. for they are Black and they are "they"
(not "him," not "her," I tell the dispatcher fourteen times, once
for each year they could lose like loose cigarettes or skittles
if wearing a hood, holding a wallet or phone). and they
have a history of mental illness, so officers see *knife!, gun!*
in every open hand. at least they live in a nice neighborhood:
single family homes on red-lined land. a world where
sergeants conduct "wellness checks" with smiles broad as arms
away from holsters. they'll even offer to remove their boots
lest they sully the foyer's imported carpet. all this is small solace
in the silence following, *thank you for your call.*
we'll send someone right over.

"...to destroy and build"

"...his life and soul are at stake in what he says
and in what is going to happen to what he says."
— Abraham J. Heschel, *The Prophets*

propelled by desert voices, the prophets
employed performance art, to spit in the face
of injustice. displays of divine harassment
to shake the conscious, chisel stone hearts.
smashing cisterns. sleeping in the street.
slicing hair with swords. eating shit-baked bread.
walking naked. I don't know what I heard —
which winds blew arid threats — but as others
donned cartoons and comic book characters,
pushed the bounds between school appropriate
and slutty, I eschewed my normal shirt and tie.
walked in the silence of a Black hoodie
and baggy blue jeans, headphones noosed
around my neck. like Abraham's children,
they were disturbed by the difference, enough
to ask *what are you?* from my slow moving hands,
they received an index card:

> *What most cops see when they pull me over.*
> *What your classmates chanted at 4 am on Snapchat.*
> *Two words.*

when asked why they can't sing "the N-Word" in rap songs

...pretend you're invited to a house party where everyone
is welcome. there's no cover charge. no expectation for you
to cop weed or beers for anyone. snacks will be provided.
at the door, the host gives you the 411:

> this is America. you can have whatever you like, do
> what you want. act like it's your birthday and forget
> all your problems. in here anything goes, almost.
> we got gin and juice to sip on, or lemonade
> if you're so inclined. if you're holding, get high
> on your own supply, but know those goons in the corner
> can get you right (but be careful: their shit's
> like playing Russian roulette with an automatic).
> furniture's been moved to make a dance floor. we've got
> more rhymes than there's cops at a Dunkin' Donuts shop.
> so shake like a polaroid picture, or simply lean back
> and enjoy the flava in your ear. if you peep The One
> who keeps on passing you by — and they're finally ready
> to let you shoot your shot when you see 'em —
> there's a private spot in the back where you can put
> your thing down, flip it and reverse it. rock it to the bang
> bang boogie. stop, drop, shut em down, open up shop. cream.
> whatever you're into. but if you're feeling out of place,
> you can call up Ali, Asher, Corey, Dave, Jaime, Malcolm,
> and definitely Marshall (them fools ain't scared to death
> or scared to look at what will be going down). basically
> only one thing's off limits when you step in my house:
> don't fuck my wife.

and if you don't know, now you know.

an open letter to the white girls caught chanting "NIGGER" on
Snapchat, again

how privileged you are the social stigma
of being a racist lingers for only a week.
that white woman tears wash away the stench
that should follow the shit still stuck to
the roof of your mouth. but it's not your fault.
you don't know that words have meanings
or histories. and it is *so unfair* that we *get to say It* —
this *reverse racism* which makes you too uncomfortable
to sing our songs outside of monochromatic parties
fueled by Sour Dabs and White Claw.
                                        but you weren't singing.
your coven chanted your "word of the night"
as if to summon Jim Crow and Judge Lynch
from their light slumber. it's our fault
you never had the ovicular fortitude to laugh-slur
in front of we who must now endure an apology
as honest as your hair compared to its roots.
and as your parents rush to protect your fragile backs
from the whips and lash of eyes as you pass
through the halls, the right whispers calling you
exactly what you are, your former teacher
has only one question — avoided by administration
cautioned by legal counsel — which "nigger"
replaced my name? replaced Chris and La Toya's?
Hannah and Timothy's? Michael and Anthony's?
Nneoma and Ashanti's? Shaniah and Ashley's?

the surprising thing

> *"...we, with love, shall force our brothers to see themselves as they are,*
> *to cease fleeing from reality and begin to change it."*
> — *The Fire Next Time*, James Baldwin

I've only been called "nigger" once by a student — at least
in my presence — and that under his breath. I wonder
if I'm doing something wrong, if it's my fault it happened
only that one time. I may need to make them more
uncomfortable with my skin or centeredness,
my uppity angry Black man way of calling spades,
pots and kettles exactly what they are. racists,
red-lining, mass incarceration, stop and frisk:
all discussed with the mandatory minimum
expectation that they consider their complicity
through complacency. yet they remain unmoved
in all the worst ways. the subtle things give me pause:
their academic ease with Shakespeare, O'Brien, and O'Connor,
how Scottish ghosts, draft-dodging Vietnam, and mass-murderers
roaming the Georgian countryside feel familiar,
yet Okonkwo, Janie, and Pecola are wholly *other* —
their stories inscrutable, lives they *can't relate to* —
their humanity opaque as the sharpie swastikas
ill-fading in our bathroom stalls, the Snapchats
of Black necks in nooses casually shared, the bombs
threating to shrapnel the mosques of classmates
they never seem to see. hidden behind expensive laptops
held together by MAGA bumper stickers, they demand
to know why a student bussed from Boston would scream
FUCK WHITE AMERICA and think it's appropriate
(he was suspended. he's still screaming: quietly,
more dangerously). and here I stand: still employed — picking cotton
from fresh aspirin bottles after every utterance
which slices a peace from my soul — and asking questions
that make them cringe. light is unsettling. like when they tell me
how their heads snapped right hearing a grandparent
— or uncle, or mother, or best friend —
topple the house of bullshit cards they built
on the "post-racial Obama-era," with a sharp exhale of breath
which revealed the truth bubbling in their heart. I ask them
about their silent response. so it was surprising, struck me as odd,
that it only happened when I told a white boy to put his phone away —
the straw that broke his fragile back. deferred his dreams.

re: thoughts on the latest racial incident(s)

on behalf of all your Black colleagues —
the three of us you can name, and the other
four you mistake us for — allow me to thank
all of you for crafting such heartfelt emails.
the time it took for you to skim the initial call
to consider the impact of racial terror on our students,
and then string together your five sentence missives
must have been so mentally taxing.

we thank you, collectively, for your comments
on how courageous you felt her message was.
we thank you for your congratulations on how
surprisingly articulate she was in writing.
we thank you for all the emotions you couldn't capture,
but still somehow managed to send: how tragic
the events. how we are all suffering, equally.
we thank you for the apologies for past silence
and complicity, your vows to *do better*
the *next time* you truly doubt will ever come.
mostly, our Ebony monolith, thanks you
for the bravely it took to specifically address
your email to one person, but then reply-all
to the entire faculty and staff.

> oh how your virtue waves before us
> like semaphore flags guiding fighter pilots
> back to the deck! how each new notification
> chime resounds like gunshots at close quarters!

when asked why I don't volunteer

because every professional development
has become an exercise in emotional sharecropping —
unpaid labor, shackled in the red-faced sun
of small groups, whipped to explain everything
they'll forget when cut off in traffic, confined
in an elevator, or too close on a sidewalk.
or worse: auction-blocked, forced to open my mouth,
show my teeth for all the assembled
after speaking simple, uncomfortable truths
in a breakout session full of buzzwords
like "equity," "inclusion," and "antiracism."
because "diversity" means "we've allowed you
to sit at our table, break our bread, become one of us —
almost," and I'd rather pick cotton than explain,
once again, that power is the number of times
you can tell your story
                        uninterrupted,
only to be ignored for the next few semesters,
centuries, or until another noose is found
in the bathroom stalls.

an open letter to those wondering why I've called this the most
racist place I've ever worked

because you're offended by the title, by the gut-punch
of Black words on a page you wish were blank,
by the accusation you feel personally implied,
as if suddenly blamed for slavery, the King assassination,
and the Clinton Crime Bill (even though your name
was never mentioned in those first 17 words).
because you're stockpiling an arsenal of responses
in a self-righteous fallout-shelter, a haven of white fragility.
because your emotional antibodies rise to fight
the wrong sickness — lymphocytes filled with *it wasn't me!*
and *how is that* my *fault?*, ignoring the cancer
exploding our community's cells. because you sent letters
of concern when a teacher called racist actions "racist."
because a committee was convened to combat the scourge
of limited student parking — disenfranchising sophomores
with new BMWs — while "nigger" remained scrawled
across art projects, campaign posters, and Snapchat.
because you minnesota-nicely told people to leave
when they complained. because your misplaced outrage
zigzags like our students of color seeing officer johnson
following them —
        through the hallway,
            through the cafeteria,
                to their classes,
                    to their bus stop,
                        to a urinal for a chat —
hand on his holster. because you're making a list of every time
you've allowed *one of them* into your car, into your home.
because your problem with Black History *Month* misses the point.
because you'll inaccurately attribute that tension in your jaw,
that burn between your shoulder blades, that breath you didn't know
you were holding. because this has all been a Rorschach Test
of your conscience, and it's clear the negative space has coalesced
into a white hoodie embossed with the words "all lives matter."

an open letter to the public school employees worried that
"antiracist" is too controversial a term

some days I believe the number of first cousins
holding hands in a marital bed is dwindling. an illusion
upended when you speak. I hope hand soap lights your face on fire and
the only available suppressant is a dull fork. I hope

termites lay oblong eggs in your pubic hair and
hone their taste for unwashed flesh. I hope your children choose your
elder care options from an old *60 Minutes* expose and

find your savings the perfect seed money for investing in
underwater solar panels. I hope happiness is a football: that you're
Charlie Brown and Time is Lucy. I hope your cat leaves, your
kite string always breaks, and ravens remember your eyes. I hope you'll

understand how you sound. I hope you realize this
poem is an acrostic — a noose waiting to tilt your neck — and act accordingly.

an open letter to my well-intentioned white educators: past,
present, and future

thank you for always seeing me as one of the good ones —
a safe bet for your efforts. a burden worth lifting. your attempts
to connect and encourage — like the educators whose movies
were mocked in the faculty lounge — didn't go unnoticed. but
I never wanted to be the first Black president. or the second.
I wasn't interested in attending Harvard or those special summer programs
sure to broaden my horizons. there's a reason why I grew tired
of Crispus Attucks, George Washington Carver, and the Rev. Dr. King
being your only assignment suggestions. why I read *Othello* while the rest
suffered through Salinger's unreliable narration. why I later asked
if you knew Sojourner Truth, Lucile Clifton, Octavia Butler —
the other dead having as much to offer. it's why my recital piece
was "Sir Duke" instead of Chopin. I know how I looked at times:
the baggy pants, the bandanna, the toothpick. the code-switching
which made you more uncomfortable than my racially charged questions.
but I can be loud without being angry, just like everybody else.
can fail without being a reflection on all who share my shade,
at least in theory. don't worry: at the time of this writing, I am not dead
or in prison. five diplomas and decades of my own students
say I turned out alright. feel free to take your share of the credit,
but understand your dreams weren't in color and I didn't need saving.

Thank You

My heartfelt thanks goes out to the good people at Sundress Publications —
especially Sherrel for being a wonderful, thoughtful Editor, and putting up
with me throughout this process — as well as all the publications which took a
chance on previous versions of these poems.

I will be forever indebted to the amazing Jackie Liu (one of my favorite people
on the planet) for creating the cover art for this collection.
https://jackieliuart.com/

A thank you for the decades of love and inspiration from my educators, my
classmates, my kids, and my colleagues, and anyone who sees themselves in
these pages, whether it is actually you or not.

Finally, to Mrs. Barbara O'Brien, "...the office secretary, she who understood/
the intersection of round pegs and square holes...," rest well; we'll have
eternity to catch up when I scoot a bigger chair up to your new desk.

Notes

Langston Hughes quotes leading the section breaks are from the poem "Theme for English B"

"a meditation on the *Desire*" – *Desire* was the first slave ship built in America and to carry Africans into Boston.

"diaspora" employs four of the principles of Kwanzaa.

"mistaken identity" references the 1989 killing of Carol Stuart by her husband, and the 1990 robbery of the Isabella Stewart Gardner Museum.

"essay for history B" is an homage to Langston Hughes' "Theme for English B."

"an open letter to an american institution" responds to Ted Kooser's "Fort Robinson."

"an open letter to my mixed little 'Sisters Who Kept Their Naturals'" is after Gwendolyn Brooks' "To Those Of My Sisters Who Kept Their Naturals."

"a confession from occupied territory" takes its title from James Baldwin's "A Report from Occupied Territory."

"when asked why they can't sing 'the N-word' in rap songs" is a test of your rap creds.

About the Author

Matthew E. Henry (MEH) is the Boston-born author of *Teaching While Black* (Main Street Rag, 2020) and *Dust & Ashes* (Californios Press, 2020). He is editor-in-chief of *The Weight Journal* which publishes the best in high school creative writing. MEH's poetry has received multiple Pushcart and Best of the Net nominations, but for some reason he continues to dabble in prose. He is an educator who received his MFA in poetry from Seattle Pacific University yet continued to spend money he didn't have completing an MA in theology and a PhD in education. His work can be found on MEHPoeting.com where he writes about education, race, religion, and burning oppressive systems to the ground.

Other Sundress Titles

Mouths of Garden
Barbara Fant
$12.99

Something Dark to Shine In
Inès Pujos
$12.99

What Nothing
Anna Meister
$12.99

Cosmobiological
Jilly Dreadful
$16.99

Slaughter the One Bird
Kimberly Ann Priest
$12.99

Sweetbitter
Stacey Balkun
$12.99

The Valley
Esteban Rodriguez
$12.99

To Everything There Is
Donna Vorreyer
$12.99

Hood Criatura
féi hernandez
$12.99

nightsong
Ever Jones
$12.99

CPSIA information can be obtained
at www.ICGtesting.com
Printed in the USA
JSHW041609090722
27802JS00005B/8